90 Days to More Faith, Freedom and Victory

Bible Devotions to Change Your Life

Faith Food Series
Volume One

Dean Wall

Scripture marked AMPLIFIED is from the Amplified® Bible, Copyright © 1954,1958,1962,1964,1965 by The Lockman Foundation.
Scripture marked BARCLAY is from The New Testament, A New Translation (William Barclay). London: Collins Clear-Type Press, 1968.
Scripture marked BBE is from The Bible In Basic English, printed in 1965 by Cambridge Press in England with no copyright.
Scripture marked BECK is from The Holy Bible In The Language of Today (William F. Beck). A.J. Holman Co, 1976.
Scripture marked CEV is from the Contemporary English Version © 1995 by American Bible Society.
Scripture marked CJB is from the Complete Jewish Bible. Copyright © 1998 by David H. Stern. Jewish New Testament Pub., Inc.
Scripture marked GWN is from GOD'S WORD® translation. Copyright © 1995 by God's Word to the Nations.
Scripture marked ICB is from the International Children's Version, New Testament. Fort Worth, TX: Sweet Publishing Company, Inc., 1983.
Scripture marked KJV is from the King James Version of the Bible.
Scripture marked LAUBACH is from The Inspired Letters In Clearest English (Frank C. Laubach). Nashville: Thomas Nelson, Inc., 1956.
Scripture marked LB is from The Living Bible, Paraphrased. Wheaton, IL: Tyndale House Publishers, 1971.
Scripture marked NASB is from the New American Standard Bible®, Copyright ©1960,1962,1963,1968,1971,1972,1973,1975, 1977,1995 by The Lockman Foundation.
Scripture marked NCV is from the International Children's Bible, New Century Version. Dallas: Word Publishing, 1988.
Scripture marked NET is from The NET Bible, Version 1.0. Copyright © 2004,2005 Biblical Studies Foundation.
Scripture marked NEW LIFE is from The New Life Testament (Gleason H. Ledyard). Canby, OR: Christian Literature Int. 1976.
Scripture marked NIV is from THE HOLY BIBLE: NEW INTERNATIONAL VERSION®. Copyright © 1973,1978,1984 by International Bible Society.
Scripture marked NJB is from the New Jerusalem Bible. Copyright © 1985, by Darton, Longman & Todd Limited and Doubleday.
Scripture marked NKJ is from The New King James Version. Copyright © 1982, Thomas Nelson, Inc.
Scripture marked NLT is from the Holy Bible, New Living Translation. Copyright © 1996, Tyndale House Publishers.
Scripture marked NRSV is from the New Revised Standard Version Bible. Copyright © 1989, Division of Christian Education of the National Council of the Churches of Christ in the United States of America.
Scripture marked PHILLIPS is from The New Testament in Modern English (J. B. Phillips). New York: The Macmillan Co., 1972.
Scripture marked RIEU is from The Four Gospels (E. V. Rieu). Harmondsworth, Middlesex: Penguin Books Ltd., 1952.
Scripture marked RSV is from the Revised Standard Version of the Bible. Copyright © 1952 [2nd edition, 1971] by the Division of Christian Education of the National Council of Churches of Christ in the United States of America.
Scripture marked SWANN is from the New Testament (George Swann). Robards, KY: George Swann Company, 1947.
Scripture marked TEV is from the Good News Bible, The Bible in Today's English Version. New York: American Bible Society, 1976.
Scripture marked THE MESSAGE is from The Message. Copyright 1993,1994,1995,1996,2000,2001, NavPress Publishing Group.
Scripture marked WEYMOUTH is from the New Testament In Modern Speech (Richard F. Weymouth). Kregel Publications, 1978.
Scripture marked WUEST is from the Wuest's Expanded Translation of the Greek New Testament (Kenneth S. Wuest). Grand Rapids: Wm. B. Eerdmans Publishing Company, 1959.
Scripture marked YLT is from the Young's Literal Translation of the Holy Bible by J.N. Young, 1862,1898.
Cover photo by Ralf Oesterwinter.

Copyright © 2009 by Dean Wall. All rights reserved.
CFA Publications
Box 702032, Tulsa, OK 74170 USA
www.CFApublications.com

Library of Congress Control Number: 2009901101
Library of Congress subject headings:
Christian life — Biblical teaching — Meditations.
Spiritual life — Christianity — Biblical teaching.
Faith — Biblical teaching — Meditations.

ISBN: 978-0-9822097-1-4

I dedicate this book to a wonderful woman,
my Mother, Elva Mae Wall.
Thank you, Mother!

Thanks

Thank you to all the faithful readers of the daily email messages I send out from www.aDevotion.org and www.ChurchForAll.org. Many of you have shared your comments and suggestions with me, which I do appreciate.

A special thanks is due to my friend Ted Pickenbrock, who has greatly helped me in making these messages better through his comments. Thank you Ted!

Contents

Introduction	11
Accept God's Acceptance	13
According To Your Faith	14
All The Promises Of God	15
All Things Are Possible	16
Be A "Do-Gooder"	17
Be A Minister	18
Be Slow To Speak	19
Cast Your Cares	20
Control Your Words	21
Declare Independence From The Devil	22
Destroyed For Lack Of Knowledge	23
Do Not Be Afraid	24
Don't Give Me What I Deserve	25
Don't Judge By Appearance	26
Don't Wait For Tomorrow	27
Don't Worry	28
Expect Favor	29
Faith And Patience	30
Faith Is The Victory	31
Fellowship With God	32
Focus On Jesus	33
Forgive Yourself	34
Give Attention To My Words	35
God's Covenant Of Words	36

God's Demonstration	37
God's Word In Your Mouth	38
God's Word Is A Seed	39
God's Word Is Settled	40
God's Word Makes You Free	41
Good Tidings Of Great Joy	42
Happy Thanksgiving!	43
Have A Happy Life	44
Have A Word Harvest	45
Heaven Is Our Home	46
Hold Fast Your Confession	47
How Does God Bless Us?	48
Keep Your Eyes On The Prize	49
Lack Of Knowledge	50
Laugh!	51
Make Friends Of Enemies	52
Make Prayer A Habit	53
Meaning Of The Resurrection	54
Open Eyes	55
Overcome Evil With Good	56
Overcome That Problem You Face	57
Overcome!	58
Pray For Our Leaders	59
Pray For Those In Authority	60
Pray Through Daily	61
Prayer Strengthens You	62
Pride And Selfishness	63
Put God First	64
Rejoice In The Lord	65
Selfishness	66
Sin Hurts	67
Sing A New Song	68
Surrounded By Favor	69
Talk To Things	70

The Benefit Of Prayer	71
The Blood Speaks	72
The Cure For Weak Faith	73
The Gift Of Righteousness	74
The Joy Of The Lord Is Your Strength	75
The Message Of Reconciliation	76
The Message Of The New Testament	77
The Ministry Of God	78
Three Keys To A Happy Marriage	79
To Become Like Jesus	80
Walk In Love	81
Watch Your Words	82
What You Say Is What You Get	83
When To Rejoice	84
When You Sin	85
Who Can Be Against Us?	86
Why Do Christians Fight So Much?	87
Why Read The Bible?	88
Words Are Spiritual Weapons	89
Words Bring Success	90
Words Control Your Life	91
You Are A Citizen of Heaven	92
You Are God's Garden	93
You Are God's Work Of Art	94
You Are Not A Failure	95
You Are Not An Orphan	96
You Are Part Of Christ's Body On Earth	97
You Can Do All Things Through Christ	98
You Don't Face Life All Alone	99
You Have A Purpose	100
Your Body Is Your House	101
Your Hairs Are Numbered	102
You Can Receive Forgiveness	103

Introduction

Originally I sent out these messages as daily emails to members of our online church at www.ChurchForAll.org. Then I realized that many did not want to join another group, yet they might enjoy and benefit from a daily email message to encourage their faith. So I started another site, just for the purpose of sending out these daily messages, at www.aDevotion.org.

The response has been very gratifying as people all over the world have continued to read these daily messages and grow stronger in faith and closer in their relationship with our wonderful Lord Jesus Christ. If you would like to receive similar messages each day by email, just go to one of the web sites mentioned above and enter your email address to be added to our list.

I am thrilled with Jesus Christ. It is my belief that everyone would love Him if they just knew Him. My quest is to help you know Him and His Word better.

Before you begin reading, I suggest you ask the Lord Jesus to open your understanding and teach you. It is always a good idea to approach God's Word with a request for God's help.

Although these messages are not perfect (because I don't know everything yet), I trust they will point you to the One who is perfect — Jesus Christ — and His Word. And that through Jesus Christ you will enjoy life as God intended.

Accept God's Acceptance

God accepts you, because of what Jesus did as your substitute, and because He loves you.

> EPHESIANS 1:6 NKJ
> 6 to the praise of the glory of His grace, by which He has made us accepted in the Beloved.

All barriers between you and God were broken down by Jesus Christ. God forgave you, and offers cleansing from all the sin you ever committed.

> 2 CORINTHIANS 5:18-21 NLT
> 18 All this newness of life is from God, who brought us back to himself through what Christ did. And God has given us the task of reconciling people to him.
> 19 For God was in Christ, reconciling the world to himself, no longer counting people's sins against them. This is the wonderful message he has given us to tell others.
> 20 We are Christ's ambassadors, and God is using us to speak to you. We urge you, as though Christ himself were here pleading with you, "Be reconciled to God!"
> 21 For God made Christ, who never sinned, to be the offering for our sin, so that we could be made right with God through Christ.

God's intention is to have a family — a loving family. He wants you to be a part of it.

> ROMANS 15:7 NCV
> 7 Christ accepted you, so you should accept each other, which will bring glory to God.

SAY THIS: *I accept that God has forgiven me and accepted me into His family.*

According To Your Faith

> MATTHEW 9:29 NKJ
> 29 Then He touched their eyes, saying, "According to your faith let it be to you."

God responds to faith.

God blesses people who have faith.

Don't you appreciate people who have faith in you? Well, God appreciates people who have faith in Him.

But His reason is not just selfish — as ours may be. God knows His ways are right and bring blessing, while protecting people from harm. So, when we have faith in God, we will follow His instructions, and the world will be a better place.

When everyone has faith in God, and follows His way of love, the world will be a perfect place.

Many people don't understand God because they think He should respond to need, instead of responding to faith.

God doesn't do that because it doesn't work. Meeting human need without them having faith in God brings no lasting benefit.

> MATTHEW 8:13 NKJ
> 13 Then Jesus said to the centurion, "Go your way; and as you have believed, so let it be done for you." And his servant was healed that same hour.

SAY THIS: *God responds to my faith.*

All The Promises Of God

2 CORINTHIANS 1:20 NCV
20 The yes to all of God's promises is in Christ, and through Christ we say yes to the glory of God.

Although the entire Bible is a message to us today, not all of it is written directly to us.

The New Testament epistles are written directly to us who are in the church, the Body of Christ, which includes all believers.

We do need to rightly divide the Bible, but since all the promises of God are yes in Christ — they find their fulfillment in Him — we can take any promise of blessing in the entire Bible and appropriate it by faith.

God has blessed us with every blessing in Christ!

EPHESIANS 1:3 NKJ
3 Blessed be the God and Father of our Lord Jesus Christ, who has blessed us with every spiritual blessing in the heavenly places in Christ,

Every promise in the Bible is not directed to us specifically. But, by faith in Jesus Christ, we can appropriate every blessing God has to offer.

When we do receive the promised blessings of God's Word, it brings glory to God.

All this is not automatic. You have to actively receive. But the main "activity" involved with receiving blessing from God is believing. To truly believe you need evidence. That's why you need to read and study the Bible.

SAY THIS: *Every Bible promise of blessing is mine in Christ.*

All Things Are Possible

> MARK 9:23 NKJ
> 23 Jesus said to him, "If you can believe, all things are possible to him who believes."

From our early years we are educated in what is impossible.

But progress continues to be made by people who attempt the impossible and achieve it.

Some have said that mankind's only real obstacle is between our two ears.

We ARE limited by what we believe, according to Jesus.

So, how can we change what we believe? Only by getting new evidence, which is available from the Word of God.

> MATTHEW 17:20 NKJ
> 20 So Jesus said to them, "Because of your unbelief; for assuredly, I say to you, if you have faith as a mustard seed, you will say to this mountain, 'Move from here to there,' and it will move; and nothing will be impossible for you.

A conventional approach will not achieve the "impossible." It will require being different from the crowd, who probably won't understand you or support you. Speaking to things and telling them to move, as Jesus taught, is certainly not conventional.

Acting differently than everyone else can be scary. It's like getting out of the boat to walk on water. But do you want conventional results?

As you read the Bible and see the instructions God gave us, you will usually find them unconventional. But the person who acts on God's Word will be blessed.

SAY THIS: *All things are possible!*

Be A "Do-Gooder"

ACTS 10:38 NKJ
38 "how God anointed Jesus of Nazareth with the Holy Spirit and with power, who went about doing good and healing all who were oppressed by the devil, for God was with Him.

Although the devil wants us to think being a "do-gooder" is bad, Jesus went about doing good. One modern translation of Acts 10:38 says that Jesus went about everywhere doing acts of kindness. That is a good example for us to follow.

Today you will have opportunity to help others — to do good. If you choose to pass up those opportunities you will miss a great blessing — not just a reward in Heaven, but also the blessing of God drawing near to you now.

Maybe you think you are too busy, or that your help would not make much difference anyway. Don't let that thinking rob you, and those God puts in your path to help, of a blessing today.

SAY THIS: *With the Lord's help, I will do good today.*

Be A Minister

2 CORINTHIANS 3:5-6 NIV
5 Not that we are competent in ourselves to claim anything for ourselves, but our competence comes from God.
6 He has made us competent as ministers of a new covenant — not of the letter but of the Spirit; for the letter kills, but the Spirit gives life.

A minister's job is turning people to God.

No one has to appoint you, ordain you, or give you credentials to make you a minister.

A minister is one who serves — serves God, and people, by turning people to God so they can receive help.

Being a minister does not require you to have a title such as pastor, bishop, or priest.

While it is true that God does call some to special places of ministry, it is a mistake to think that we all cannot, or should not, minister.

A minister is a middle-man like a real estate agent. A person can find out about God on their own with a Bible, just like someone can buy a house directly, but it is easier and faster to have a more experienced person who knows the territory help you.

Someone who helps another is a minister. You can do that.

SAY THIS: *God made me able to minister — to help someone.*

Be Slow To Speak

JAMES 1:19 NIV
19 My dear brothers, take note of this: Everyone should be quick to listen, slow to speak and slow to become angry,

How many times have you said something and later regretted it?

Too often we practice: Speak now and think later.

What would happen if you silently consulted with God before speaking? If you thought about, and prayed about, everything you said — before you said it — your life would be different.

1 PETER 3:10 LB
10 If you want a happy, good life, keep control of your tongue, and guard your lips from telling lies.

Words are powerful and should be used to accomplish a purpose. Don't just talk for no reason.

PROVERBS 17:28 NIV
28 Even a fool is thought wise if he keeps silent, and discerning if he holds his tongue.

Remember, you can always learn more by listening than you can by talking.

Be slow to speak!

SAY THIS: *God, please help me to control my tongue.*

Cast Your Cares

1 PETER 5:7 AMPLIFIED
7 Casting the whole of your care — all your anxieties, all your worries, all your concerns, once and for all — on Him; for He cares for you affectionately, and cares about you watchfully.

God is not just mildly interested in you. He cares for you just as a good mother cares for her infant child — affectionately and watchfully.

Would it be reasonable for a well-loved infant to worry? Neither is it reasonable for you to worry when God loves you and has promised to take care of you.

To worry you must believe one of two lies: God can't take care of you, or God won't take care of you.

PHILIPPIANS 4:6-7 NRSV
6 Do not worry about anything, but in everything by prayer and supplication with thanksgiving let your requests be made known to God.
7 And the peace of God, which surpasses all understanding, will guard your hearts and your minds in Christ Jesus.

Worry is not appropriate for a child of God.

SAY THIS: *I throw all my cares on God because He cares for me.*

Control Your Words

1 PETER 4:11 NIV
11 If anyone speaks, he should do it as one speaking the very words of God . . . .

When you speak what the Bible says, you are speaking the very words of God. Anything contrary to what the Bible says, should never be spoken by a Christian.

EPHESIANS 4:29 NIV
29 Do not let any unwholesome talk come out of your mouths, but only what is helpful for building others up according to their needs, that it may benefit those who listen.

JAMES 4:11 NKJ
11 Do not speak evil of one another . . . .

TITUS 3:2 NKJ
2 to speak evil of no one . . . .

You are responsible for what you say. If you cannot say something good, the Bible is clear: keep quiet.

SAY THIS: *Lord please help me to keep quiet unless I have something to say that would be acceptable to you.*

Declare Independence From The Devil

Just as it is sometimes necessary for people to declare their freedom from the tyranny of earthly rulers, so we must declare and enforce our spiritual freedom — purchased for us by the precious blood of our wonderful Lord Jesus Christ.

> COLOSSIANS 1:13-14 NKJ
> 13 He has delivered us from the power of darkness and conveyed us into the kingdom of the Son of His love,
> 14 in whom we have redemption through His blood, the forgiveness of sins.

The devil is defeated. Jesus already won the battle. You have been delivered from the power and authority of the prince of darkness. Jesus has made you truly free.

> JOHN 8:36 NKJ
> 36 "Therefore if the Son makes you free, you shall be free indeed.

But to fully enjoy the freedom that is yours through the sacrifice of Jesus Christ, you must proclaim your freedom. You cannot keep silent, but must speak forth and declare that you are free from the hand of the enemy!

> PSALM 107:2 NKJ
> 2 Let the redeemed of the Lord say so, whom He has redeemed from the hand of the enemy,

SAY THIS: *I am free from the devil's control. The devil has no power over me. Jesus is my Lord.*

Day Eleven

Destroyed For Lack Of Knowledge

HOSEA 4:6 KJV
6 My people are destroyed for lack of knowledge . . . .

Are people's lives destroyed because God does not love them? Do people come to ruin and live in misery because God is callous and uncaring?

NO!

People are destroyed for lack of knowledge — even God's people. What kind of knowledge? Knowledge that is available in the Bible: how to walk in faith, how to overcome, how to get prayers answered, how to resist the devil, etc.

God is not to blame for our troubles. God has already made provision for us. But we must avail ourselves of what God has provided.

How can we benefit from God's great provision if we don't even know about it? So, we should seek the knowledge of God on our own, and receive teaching from others, also.

There is not one among us who does not have much to learn. No one yet is walking in the absolute fullness of what God has provided.

This must be one of the saddest verses in the Bible. To think that God's people are destroyed simply because of a lack of knowledge. As God's children, they are our brothers and sisters. It is our relatives being destroyed, and we should do what we can to stop it.

Let's quit giving place to the devil by our lack of knowledge of God's Word. And, as we learn from God's Word we should share our knowledge with others, so they can walk in freedom and victory, too.

SAY THIS: *I will study God's Word so I can know the truth and not let the devil destroy me for lack of knowledge.*

Do Not Be Afraid

> JOSHUA 1:9 NKJ
> 9 "Have I not commanded you? Be strong and of good courage; do not be afraid, nor be dismayed, for the Lord your God is with you wherever you go."

Over and over the Bible tells us to not be afraid.

When you stop and think about it — it's ridiculous to be afraid when God is with you — and for you.

As humans, we tend to forget. Maybe that's why God said so many times to "Fear not!"

Here are just a couple examples.

> LUKE 12:7 NIV
> 7 Indeed, the very hairs of your head are all numbered. Don't be afraid; you are worth more than many sparrows.

> ISAIAH 41:13 NIV
> 13 For I am the LORD, your God, who takes hold of your right hand and says to you, Do not fear; I will help you.

SAY THIS: *I will not be afraid because I trust in God, who is with me.*

Don't Give Me What I Deserve

Do you really want what you deserve? Maybe you should first find out what you really deserve.

> PSALM 103:8-10 NIV
> 8 The LORD is compassionate and gracious, slow to anger, abounding in love.
> 9 He will not always accuse, nor will he harbor his anger forever;
> 10 he does not treat us as our sins deserve or repay us according to our iniquities.

Thank God that I don't get what I deserve! People clamoring to get what they deserve are really in the dark.

God is the judge and He declares that we have all fallen short — none of us deserves good. But the wonderful news is that God loves us so much that He is not giving us what we deserve. But it doesn't stop there. It gets better. Believers are actually going to receive what Jesus deserves!

Jesus took what we deserved — punishment. And now, because of His great love, offers us what He deserves — freely as a gift of love.

How can you not respond to Someone like that!

SAY THIS: *Thank You, Lord for not giving me what I deserve, but being merciful and gracious and giving me what you deserve instead.*

Don't Judge By Appearance

JOHN 7:24 NKJ
24 "Do not judge according to appearance, but judge with righteous judgment."

Making a snap judgment based on appearance often works — but not always. And the exceptions can really cost you.

The world teaches us to judge people by their appearance. But God doesn't judge people by how they look — and neither should we.

1 SAMUEL 16:7 NLT
7 But the LORD said to Samuel, "Don't judge by his appearance or height, for I have rejected him. The LORD doesn't make decisions the way you do! People judge by outward appearance, but the LORD looks at a person's thoughts and intentions."

One main reason we're not qualified to judge others is because we don't know their thoughts and intentions. Only God does.

As they say, "You can't always judge a book by its cover."

LUKE 16:15 CEV
15 But Jesus told them: You are always making yourselves look good, but God sees what is in your heart. The things that most people think are important are worthless as far as God is concerned.

It is important that we treat all people with respect — since they are created and loved by God — no matter how they look.

SAY THIS: *Lord, help me to not judge people by their appearance.*

Don't Wait For Tomorrow

PROVERBS 27:1 NIV
1 Do not boast about tomorrow, for you do not know what a day may bring forth.

Do what you need to do today.

Don't wait to receive Jesus. Don't put off doing the will of God. Don't wait to tell someone you love them.

JAMES 4:13-15 NIV
13 Now listen, you who say, "Today or tomorrow we will go to this or that city, spend a year there, carry on business and make money."
14 Why, you do not even know what will happen tomorrow. What is your life? You are a mist that appears for a little while and then vanishes.
15 Instead, you ought to say, "If it is the Lord's will, we will live and do this or that."

You don't know what tomorrow holds — or even if you will be here tomorrow.

Keep your focus on God. Trust in Him, and do His will today.

SAY THIS: *I will do what God leads me to do today.*

Don't Worry

> 1 PETER 5:7 NLT
> 7 Give all your worries and cares to God, for he cares about what happens to you.

Probably the biggest temptation most believers face is the temptation to worry.

What is worry? Worry is thinking that leaves God out. Worry is the opposite of faith. Instead of expecting God's help — you expect the worst.

> 1 PETER 5:7 CEV
> 7 God cares for you, so turn all your worries over to him.

The Bible has much to say about not worrying. Worry is not appropriate for a child of God.

> MATTHEW 6:32 CEV
> 32 Only people who don't know God are always worrying about such things. Your Father in heaven knows that you need all of these.

> PHILIPPIANS 4:6 ICB
> 6 Do not worry about anything. But pray and ask God for everything you need. And when you pray, always give thanks.

SAY THIS: *I will not worry. I will trust in God. He will take care of me and everything that concerns me.*

Expect Favor

> PSALM 5:12 NIV
> 12 For surely, O LORD, you bless the righteous; you surround them with your favor as with a shield.

If Jesus is your Lord, then He is also your righteousness (1 Corinthians 1:30, Romans 5:17). So, you are righteous in Christ and qualify for this blessing.

Favor is the blessing of God causing people to like you and treat you well.

Why expect favor?

Because God is your Father. He loves you. And He responds to faith. When you walk in faith you expect blessings.

> PROVERBS 16:7 NIV
> 7 When a man's ways are pleasing to the LORD, he makes even his enemies live at peace with him.

Some people always talk of how badly they are treated and how things always go wrong for them. Should we be surprised? After all, Jesus told us in Mark 11:23 that we would have what we say.

Why not begin to say that God surrounds your life with favor?

SAY THIS: *I expect God's favor in my life.*

Faith And Patience

> HEBREWS 6:12 NKJ
> 12 that you do not become sluggish, but imitate those who through faith and patience inherit the promises.

Patience is not just putting up with things.

Patience means to continue, to persevere, to stay steady, to maintain your course, to not grow weary in doing good and quit.

Patience is a fruit of the spirit, so to walk in Bible patience you must keep your spiritual life strong, by feeding on the Word and fellowshiping with God.

We receive from God by faith, but our faith has to be undergirded by patience to possess and enjoy His promises.

It's normal for there to be a time of waiting and testing when we believe the promises of God. But hang on to your faith and it will see you through.

> JAMES 5:10-11 NIV
> 10 Brothers, as an example of patience in the face of suffering, take the prophets who spoke in the name of the Lord.
> 11 As you know, we consider blessed those who have persevered. You have heard of Job's perseverance and have seen what the Lord finally brought about. The Lord is full of compassion and mercy.

God's Word will come to pass in your life. Don't quit believing.

Hang in there!

SAY THIS: *I will imitate those who through faith and patience inherit the promises of God.*

Faith Is The Victory

1 JOHN 5:4 NKJ
4 For whatever is born of God overcomes the world. And this is the victory that has overcome the world — our faith.

We all love to win.

Victory is sweet. One reason it's so sweet is that it's usually not easy. Victory takes effort — often great effort.

Effort is also required in the spiritual battle of good against evil we are all engaged in. But the effort required of us is to maintain our attitude of faith in God and His Word.

We cannot overcome the strategies of the devil by our willpower, or by our own strength. We must use the spiritual weapons God has provided for us.

As a child of God — you are a winner! The victory is already yours through what Jesus Christ did on your behalf. Don't let the enemy steal the victory away from you.

Your enemy comes to steal your faith. Don't let it happen.

SAY THIS: *I overcome and walk in victory by my faith in God.*

Fellowship With God

> 1 CORINTHIANS 1:9 NIV
> 9 God, who has called you into fellowship with his Son Jesus Christ our Lord, is faithful.

You need to stop and think about this. God wants to have fellowship with you.

We are not talking about some lower level person. Not just a leader of a country. Not just a billionaire.

God!

Stop and think about God, all His knowledge, all His wealth, all His power — the ruler of the Universe, and all that He could choose to do.

Why would God desire your company?

Honestly, I don't know. All I can say is that He does, according to the Bible.

But what an opportunity! What a privilege! To fellowship with GOD!

What does fellowship mean? The word used in 1 Corinthians 1:9 is the Greek word "koinonia" (koy-nohn-ee'-ah). Some meanings are fellowship, association, communion, participation, intimacy, partnership, and a having in common.

That is what God wants with you. Koinonia.

The same word is used in the following verse. Notice how the Living Bible translates it.

> 2 CORINTHIANS 13:14 LB
> 14 May the grace of our Lord Jesus Christ be with you all. May God's love and the Holy Spirit's friendship be yours. Paul

SAY THIS: *I will respond to God's call and fellowship with Him.*

Focus On Jesus

True Christianity is not a religion based on rules and rituals, but a living relationship with Jesus Christ.

Many people reduce Christianity down to attending church meetings and trying not to commit a list of certain sins.

But being a Christian is being united with Jesus, a member of His body, with His life in your heart.

Jesus should be your focus — not religious activity — but the person of Jesus, the Lord and Christ.

> 1 CORINTHIANS 1:9 NIV
> 9 God, who has called you into fellowship with his Son Jesus Christ our Lord, is faithful.

Church meetings, Bible reading, etc. can be good, but should not be allowed to become an end in themselves. They are tools to help us know Jesus and walk more closely with Him.

The Bible says we are to be faithful; but faithful to what: a religious system, an organization — or, a Person? Are you serving Jesus — or serving something else as His substitute?

The focus of your life should be to please Jesus.

> COLOSSIANS 1:18 NRSV
> 18 He is the head of the body, the church; he is the beginning, the firstborn from the dead, so that he might come to have first place in everything.

Does Jesus have first place in your life? In your schedule? If not, why not?

In everything, Jesus should be central.

SAY THIS: *I will keep my focus on Jesus Christ.*

Forgive Yourself

> 1 JOHN 2:12 NLT
> 12 I am writing to you who are God's children because your sins have been forgiven through Jesus.
>
> COLOSSIANS 3:13 NIV
> 13 . . . Forgive as the Lord forgave you.
>
> GALATIANS 5:14 NIV
> 14 The entire law is summed up in a single command: "Love your neighbor as yourself."

For many people, the hardest person to forgive is themselves.

If God can forgive us, then we can, and must, forgive ourselves. Not to forgive ourselves is to exalt ourselves above God.

If God can decree that we are forgive-able, but we say we are too bad to be forgiven, we are saying we know more than God.

Should your standards be higher than God's standards? He forgives. Why won't you forgive yourself?

The devil wants you to stay focused on your past and your failures, so you will not receive God's blessing.

God wants you to believe His Word and focus on His victory so you will have a better future.

Which one will you choose to follow?

SAY THIS: *Because God has forgiven me, I forgive myself.*

Give Attention To My Words

PROVERBS 4:20-22 NKJ
20 My son, give attention to my words; Incline your ear to my sayings.
21 Do not let them depart from your eyes; Keep them in the midst of your heart;
22 For they are life to those who find them, And health to all their flesh.

Giving attention to God's Word is not as easy as it once was. Today we have a multitude of distractions. Busyness seems to be a disease shared by everyone. We all have more than we can do.

Yet . . .

God doesn't change. His Word doesn't change. It still says the same thing it did a thousand years ago — and it will still say the same thing a thousand years from now.

"Give attention to my words . . . ."

We are confronted with a choice. What is most important? To what shall we give our limited time? God, or . . . ?

God makes promises no one else does — or can. He created, so He knows how things work.

Life. Life in its fullness. Life as God intended it to be. And health. Isn't that what everyone would like? That is the written guarantee offered by God to the human race — for paying attention to what He has said.

SAY THIS: *I choose to pay attention to God's Word. I choose life and health. I choose God.*

God's Covenant Of Words

> ISAIAH 59:21 NKJ
> 21 "As for Me," says the Lord, "this is My covenant with them: My Spirit who is upon you, and My words which I have put in your mouth, shall not depart from your mouth, nor from the mouth of your descendants, nor from the mouth of your descendants' descendants," says the Lord, "from this time and forevermore."

According to Isaiah 59:21, part of our covenant with God includes continually having His words in our mouth and in the mouth of our descendants. Not only are we to speak God's Word, but we are to train our descendants to do the same.

God must know something about the importance of the words we speak, that we have not yet understood.

Although a growing number of believers are beginning to realize the importance of the words we speak, the vast majority of Christians have never heard any teaching on this subject. Yet, if you search the Bible, you will see that God puts a major emphasis on what we say.

> 1 PETER 4:11 NIV
> 11 If anyone speaks, he should do it as one speaking the very words of God . . . .

Look at the Bible for yourself. Decide for yourself. You will surely decide that the Bible teaches that believers should speak words in agreement with what God says.

What you say IS important.

SAY THIS: *I will speak words in agreement with what God has said, and I will teach my descendants to do likewise.*

God's Demonstration

ROMANS 5:8 NKJ
8 But God demonstrates His own love toward us, in that while we were still sinners, Christ died for us.

There is no reason to say, "If God loves me, let Him prove it!" He already has.

God gave a demonstration proving He loves you at Calvary — where Jesus died a cruel death on a cross. He died, in your place, suffering punishment you deserved, to set you free.

By dying for you, God proved He loved you supremely. How could He love you more?

Jesus showed that He loves you more than He loves Himself.

JOHN 15:13 NKJ
13 "Greater love has no one than this, than to lay down one's life for his friends.

Jesus gave His life for you. What more could He do?

1 JOHN 3:16a NKJ
16 By this we know love, because He laid down His life for us.

Many people have a distorted view of God. The true picture of God's nature is that He loves all the people of the world so much, He was willing to suffer for their freedom.

SAY THIS: *God loves me — and He proved it!*

God's Word In Your Mouth

EPHESIANS 6:17 NIV
17 Take the helmet of salvation and the sword of the Spirit, which is the word of God.

The sword, or weapon, of the spirit is speaking the Word of God. Left sitting in a book on your shelf, it does you no good.

A weapon must be used against an adversary to be of any benefit. Our adversary is the devil and a weapon he uses is doubt. We must speak God's Word to actively resist doubt, so it won't defeat us.

JAMES 1:22 NIV
22 Do not merely listen to the word, and so deceive yourselves. Do what it says.

We need to personalize the Bible, and act on it. The first, and main, way to accomplish this is to speak in agreement with what the Bible says.

For a short basic confession to get you started, look at www.believers.org/helps/basiccon.htm

SAY THIS: *I take the sword of the spirit and put it in my mouth by speaking in agreement with the Word of God.*

God's Word Is A Seed

Most people expect God's Word to work like a stick of dynamite — but Jesus told us God's Word is like a seed.

> LUKE 8:11 NKJ
> 11 "Now the parable is this: The seed is the word of God.

The Holy Spirit, through Peter, also said God's Word is a seed.

> 1 PETER 1:23 NKJ
> 23 having been born again, not of corruptible seed but incorruptible, through the word of God which lives and abides forever,

God's Word is alive. Just like a seed — the Bible is full of unseen life.

> JOHN 6:63 ICB
> 63 It is not the flesh that gives a person life. It is the spirit that gives life. The words I told you are spirit, and so they give life.

Jesus said His words are alive. They contain life, so they give life. The words in your Bible may look lifeless and powerless. Seeds do, also. But they are not without life or power.

In Mark 4:30-31, Jesus explained that the kingdom of God works like a seed. So, if we are to understand God's kingdom and how He operates, we need to understand seeds.

SAY THIS: *God's Word is good seed. I will plant it in my life and it will bring forth a good harvest.*

God's Word Is Settled

> PSALM 119:89 NKJ
> 89 Forever, O Lord, Your word is settled in heaven.

Heaven is not running around trying to figure out the will of God. His Word is settled in Heaven.

God surely had enough time before the Bible was written down to make any changes in His plans. Now that He has given His Word, He will keep it and see that it comes to pass.

> MARK 13:31 NKJ
> 31 "Heaven and earth will pass away, but My words will by no means pass away."

> ISAIAH 40:8 NKJ
> 8 "The grass withers, the flower fades, but the word of our God stands forever."

> 1 PETER 1:23 NKJ
> 23 having been born again, not of corruptible seed but incorruptible, through the word of God which lives and abides forever,

> JOHN 17:17 NKJ
> 17 "Sanctify them by Your truth. Your word is truth.

The issue is settled in Heaven. Now you should settle it: God's Word is true. God said what He meant and meant what He said.

SAY THIS: *God tells the truth, so I will not doubt what He has said.*

God's Word Makes You Free

JOHN 8:31-32 NRSV
31 Then Jesus said to the Jews who had believed in him, "If you continue in my word, you are truly my disciples;
32 and you will know the truth, and the truth will make you free."

Many people think God's Word will put them into bondage. (I used to think that.) Like most of the world's ideas, this is opposite to the truth.

A major reason people go their own way instead of turning to Jesus Christ is because they think following Him and His Word will restrict them and keep them from enjoying life. What a deception!

The only way to know true freedom in this life is found through the Word of God: the Bible.

Also notice that the "truth" Jesus refers to is found in His Word. Just knowing any "truth" does not guarantee freedom.

If you desire freedom, you now know the guaranteed formula to achieve it. Will you follow the directions?

SAY THIS: *I will continue in the message of Jesus Christ. As I do I will know the truth. As I act on that truth it will make me free.*

Good Tidings Of Great Joy

LUKE 2:10-11 NKJ
10 Then the angel said to them, "Do not be afraid, for behold, I bring you good tidings of great joy which will be to all people.
11 "For there is born to you this day in the city of David a Savior, who is Christ the Lord.

What kind of statement was this? "Great joy . . . to all people."?

Billions of people — maybe two out of three on earth — have never even heard the "Gospel of Jesus Christ," or good news, as the term gospel means.

Is this really for all people?

Yes, and we are supposed to tell them. God is a Savior — one who delivers and makes whole.

The true message of God is really good news. The kind of news that people will get excited about when they truly understand it.

If you say, "I don't see what there is to get so excited about," then you don't yet understand the Gospel.

We are dealing with "good tidings of GREAT JOY — which will be to all people."

"So what's so great about it?"

Being made right with God as a free gift. Being set free from the bondage of sin. Being delivered from the curse, including sickness, poverty, and spiritual death. Being given new life and brought into God's own family. Knowing that God is your father and your friend . . . and so much more!

SAY THIS: *I have received Good News that will make people have great joy!*

Happy Thanksgiving!

PSALM 107:1 NKJ
1 Oh, give thanks to the Lord, for He is good! For His mercy endures forever.

While we all have much to be thankful for, it is easy to lose the right perspective.

God's Word helps us keep the right perspective. We deserve God's wrath and punishment. But instead we are offered His grace, mercy, and love. Not only that, but He has blessed us with every spiritual blessing in Christ Jesus and has given us richly all things to enjoy (Ephesians 1:3, 1 Timothy 6:17).

You do have much to be thankful for.

Things could probably be better in your life. But certainly they could be a lot worse.

No doubt you have heard the line, "I complained about having no shoes, until I saw a man with no feet . . ."

Remember this secret: you will never be happy without being thankful. Also, practicing thankfulness will make you happy.

So, the key to being happy is to be thankful.

SAY THIS: *I will be happy when I give thanks.*

Have A Happy Life

1 PETER 3:10-11 NLT
10 For the Scriptures say, "If you want a happy life and good days, keep your tongue from speaking evil, and keep your lips from telling lies.
11 Turn away from evil and do good. Work hard at living in peace with others.

Why just tolerate life when you can have a happy life?

Obviously, you have some choice in the matter, according to these verses. So, make the obvious choice, and ask God to help you.

Notice that the first instructions given in these verses concern the words you speak.

What you say is enormously important, according to the Bible. Yet, most believers are unaware of the importance Scripture places on the words they speak.

Why not ask God right now to help you understand and apply this instruction, so you can reap the benefits?

SAY THIS: *Thank you Lord for giving me a happy life and good days. Thank you for helping me not to speak evil or tell lies. Thank you for helping me to avoid evil, do good, and live in peace.*

Have A Word Harvest

JOSHUA 1:8 NIV
8 Do not let this Book of the Law depart from your mouth; meditate on it day and night, so that you may be careful to do everything written in it. Then you will be prosperous and successful.

When God first gave anyone instructions for success, the first thing He said was to always keep His Word on their lips.

Jesus taught that God's Word was a seed (Luke 8:11). Seed produces a harvest — if used properly.

The harvest that God's Word produces in your life is freedom (John 8:31-32). Here are three steps to seeing a harvest of freedom in your life:

1. Plant the seed of the Word by reading it, saying it, and hearing it.

2. Water the seed by reading, speaking, and hearing the Word some more.

3. Gather the harvest by speaking the Word (when you believe it and know it inwardly).

Most people try to skip the first two steps. No wonder they have not had better results! You cannot reap the harvest without planting the seed and watering it.

Feed your faith, in every area you desire to be strong in, by speaking God's Word that covers those subjects.

Remember — if you want to harvest a continuous crop of freedom — you must plant the seed of God's Word continuously.

SAY THIS: *I will read, speak, and listen to God's Word.*

Heaven Is Our Home

PHILIPPIANS 3:20 LB
20 But our homeland is in heaven, where our Savior, the Lord Jesus Christ, is; and we are looking forward to his return from there.

Heaven is a real place. In fact, Heaven is ultimate reality. There are real people there, involved in real activities. But most importantly, our wonderful Lord Jesus Christ and our Father God are there.

Sometimes people talk of someone who has departed this life as "having gone to their reward."

Heaven is not a reward.

There will be rewards given out by God, but going to Heaven is not a reward. Heaven is a return to normal.

That's right. Heaven is the way life was supposed to be. Heaven is normal. What we have been experiencing on this sin-infested planet is sub-normal.

But part of the Good News is that Jesus will not leave this place, or us, sub-normal forever. One day, maybe soon, Jesus will return from Heaven and change things on Earth back to what God intended when He created this place.

Everything on Earth, as originally created, was a reflection of the home planet, Heaven. All the beauty and everything good that we enjoy on Earth is but a dim reflection of what Heaven offers.

What makes Heaven our home? Home is where your family is. Home is where you are comfortable. Home is where you have a place to live. Home is where you belong. For the believer in Jesus Christ, Heaven fits all those descriptions.

SAY THIS: *Heaven is my home.*

Day Thirty-Five

Hold Fast Your Confession

HEBREWS 3:1; 4:14 NKJ
1 Therefore, holy brethren, partakers of the heavenly calling, consider the Apostle and High Priest of our confession, Christ Jesus,
14 Seeing then that we have a great High Priest who has passed through the heavens, Jesus the Son of God, let us hold fast our confession.

HEBREWS 10:23 NKJ
23 Let us hold fast the confession of our hope without wavering, for He who promised is faithful.

Your confession is what you say. You should persistently continue speaking in faith, agreeing with what God has said, regardless of circumstances. If it never seemed like it was not working, there would be no need to hold fast, or hang on, to a confession of faith.

Some people are surprised when they act on God's Word and it does not immediately come to pass. But there is abundant evidence in Scripture showing that is normal. God never promised that everything would happen instantly. The time period involved gives us opportunity to walk in faith and please God.

Remember that authority is released through words. When we speak in DIS-agreement with what God says, we are giving authority in that area of our lives to our enemy. This is why Scripture tells us to struggle (if necessary) to keep speaking in agreement with God's Word.

Why does the Bible tell us to "hold fast" — or you might say "hang on tight" or "hang on for dear life." Obviously, something or someone is trying hard to get us to turn loose. Who or what do you think that is?

SAY THIS: *With God's help, I will keep speaking in agreement with the Word of God, no matter what the circumstances may say.*

How Does God Bless Us?

Does God bless us by giving us everything we think we should have, even if it's bad for us?

Does God bless us by always letting us have our way — whether it's the best way for us, or not?

Does God bless us by letting us get away with self-destructive behavior?

Does God bless us by letting us mistreat other people with impunity?

Does God bless us by giving us more responsibility, more money, or more fame, than we can handle?

Does God bless us by allowing us to never face the consequences of our actions?

Does God bless us by never allowing us to struggle or overcome difficulty?

If God blessed us in any of those ways, He would not be a good Father.

God blesses us by changing us into what we should be. He makes us to BE a blessing. That puts us into God's category, where we can enjoy fellowship with Him — which is the greatest blessing.

> GENESIS 12:2 NIV
> 2 "I will make you into a great nation and I will bless you; I will make your name great, and you will be a blessing.

SAY THIS: *Thank you Lord for your blessing.*

Keep Your Eyes On The Prize

PHILIPPIANS 3:14 KJV
14 I press toward the mark for the prize of the high calling of God in Christ Jesus.

What will really matter at the end of your life on earth?

Will what you are giving attention to now still be important then?

Or, will you be filled with regret for what you did — or didn't do?

Distractions abound. TV, phone calls, web sites, books, movies.

It might be a good idea to stop and evaluate how you are investing your time.

1 CORINTHIANS 9:24 NIV
24 Do you not know that in a race all the runners run, but only one gets the prize? Run in such a way as to get the prize.

Run to win. Win what?

The true prize is to know God intimately and be His friend.

2 CORINTHIANS 4:18 NIV
18 So we fix our eyes not on what is seen, but on what is unseen. For what is seen is temporary, but what is unseen is eternal.

One day, possibly soon, you will stand before God. Why not order your life now based on that "final reckoning?"

A wise person would not invest everything in something temporary. A wise person invests in something that will last.

Invest your life wisely!

SAY THIS: *Lord, help me to keep my eyes on what is important and lasting.*

Lack Of Knowledge

HOSEA 4:6a NKJ
6 My people are destroyed for lack of knowledge.

People wonder why many Christians experience so much trouble in life, instead of victory. The reason, according to the Bible, is a lack of knowledge.

The Bible tells us the devil is out to destroy us, but it also makes clear that we can overcome his attacks. The real problem lies with our ignorance. Real knowledge produces faith. When we really know something, we have faith in it. Then we will act on that knowledge.

The reason God's people are destroyed by calamity is not because God doesn't love us, or because God is not able to help us. It is simply that we don't know the truth. If we really knew the truth, we would act on that knowledge. Acting on true knowledge makes you free — it does not destroy you or put you into bondage.

JOHN 8:31-32 NKJ
31 Then Jesus said to those Jews who believed Him, "If you abide in My word, you are My disciples indeed.
32 "And you shall know the truth, and the truth shall make you free."

God's Word is our instruction book. When we act on it, things will work for us. God allows us to make choices. When we make the right choices, we will be blessed.

Don't let the devil condemn you with this message. Instead, let it give you hope. You can learn God's Word and act on it more accurately in the future — and be blessed!

SAY THIS: *God gave me the knowledge in the Bible so I could know the truth, act on it, and be blessed.*

Laugh!

PSALM 2:4 KJV
4 He that sitteth in the heavens shall laugh: the Lord shall have them in derision.

PSALM 37:13 KJV
13 The Lord shall laugh at him: for he seeth that his day is coming.

PSALM 59:8 KJV
8 But thou, O LORD, shalt laugh at them; thou shalt have all the heathen in derision.

ECCLESIASTES 3:4 KJV
4 A time to weep, and a time to laugh; a time to mourn, and a time to dance;

LUKE 6:21 KJV
21 Blessed are ye that hunger now: for ye shall be filled. Blessed are ye that weep now: for ye shall laugh.

PROVERBS 17:22 KJV
22 A merry heart doeth good like a medicine: but a broken spirit drieth the bones.

God laughs. So should you!

SAY THIS: *I will laugh with God today.*

Make Friends Of Enemies

PROVERBS 25:21-22 LB
21-22 If your enemy is hungry, give him food! If he is thirsty, give him something to drink! This will make him feel ashamed of himself, and God will reward you.

Why would anyone want to be an enemy of someone who treated them well?

Your actions should cause your enemy to reconsider being your enemy.

When you treat your enemies well, not only do you have a good chance of making them friends, but also God will reward you.

ROMANS 12:19-21 LB
19 Dear friends, never avenge yourselves. Leave that to God, for he has said that he will repay those who deserve it. [Don't take the law into your own hands.]
20 Instead, feed your enemy if he is hungry. If he is thirsty give him something to drink and you will be "heaping coals of fire on his head." In other words, he will feel ashamed of himself for what he has done to you.
21 Don't let evil get the upper hand, but conquer evil by doing good.

The way to turn an enemy into a friend is to treat them in a friendly manner.

This is God's plan. It should be your plan, too.

SAY THIS: *Treat enemies like friends and you won't have any enemies.*

Day Forty-One

Make Prayer A Habit

ROMANS 12:12 NRSV
12 Rejoice in hope, be patient in suffering, persevere in prayer.

Prayer is a habit that, like every other good habit, must be developed.

You know you need to pray. You need God's help, His wisdom and His guidance. But you must persevere in prayer. The activities of life try to keep you from praying. So persevere!

LUKE 21:36 BBE
36 But keep watch at all times with prayer, that you may be strong enough to come through all these things and take your place before the Son of man.

In communing with God, you gain strength that comes in no other way. You find the wisdom and courage to face life and overcome.

1 THESSALONIANS 5:17-18 ICB
17 Never stop praying.
18 Give thanks whatever happens. That is what God wants for you in Christ Jesus.

Learn to always include God in your thoughts. Ask Him about everything. Cultivate your relationship by continual communication. And one of the most important things for you to communicate to God is your gratitude. Thank God for everything.

Don't relegate prayer to just when you're on your knees. As you go about your activities, include God by constant communion with Him.

Talk to God about everything!

SAY THIS: *Lord, help me to develop the habit of continual communication with you.*

Meaning Of The Resurrection

The resurrection of Jesus of Nazareth was the greatest event in human history.

Why?

Not just because someone came back from death. That had happened before.

Jesus was acting as a representative for the human race. What He was doing was not for Himself — but for us.

> ROMANS 4:25 NKJ
> 25 who was delivered up because of our offenses, and was raised because of our justification.

The people watching Jesus die on the cross knew nothing of this. Later it was revealed what actually happened. Jesus was being a substitute for the human race, suffering in our stead. When divine justice was satisfied — Jesus was raised from the dead as your representative. You got credit for what Jesus did.

It was not just the death and resurrection of one man. It was the legal death and resurrection of us all. All Jesus did was as mankind's substitute representative.

Jesus was not raised from the dead until you were justified. That means declared righteous, or in right standing with God.

The resurrection of Jesus, according to Scripture, is a declaration that God has taken care of the sin problem and made you righteous.

SAY THIS: *Father, please help me to understand the implications of the resurrection of Jesus Christ in my life.*

Open Eyes

> 2 KINGS 6:17 NKJ
> 17 And Elisha prayed, and said, "Lord, I pray, open his eyes that he may see." Then the Lord opened the eyes of the young man, and he saw. And behold, the mountain was full of horses and chariots of fire all around Elisha.

What we see with our physical eyes is not all that's happening.

Spiritual forces are active around us. Unless God "opens our eyes" we're in the dark to what's really happening.

Of course, it shouldn't be necessary for us to "see" into the spirit realm to believe what God has said, such as that His angels would keep charge of us always to protect us.

> ACTS 26:18 NKJ
> 18 'to open their eyes and to turn them from darkness to light, and from the power of Satan to God, that they may receive forgiveness of sins and an inheritance among those who are sanctified by faith in Me.'

When God told Paul what his calling was, the first step mentioned was "to open their eyes . . . that they may receive."

For us to receive all that God has provided for us, we must also have "our eyes opened."

Our prayer needs to be that of the Psalmist.

> PSALM 119:18 NKJ
> 18 Open my eyes, that I may see wondrous things from Your law.

SAY THIS: *Lord, open my eyes. Give me understanding and insight.*

Overcome Evil With Good

ROMANS 12:21 NIV
21 Do not be overcome by evil, but overcome evil with good.

There seems to be no lack of evil. That gives us an opportunity to overcome.

We will be tempted to respond in kind — to strike back at those who hurt us. But that is a bad choice. All it leads to is more pain and misery for more people — including ourselves.

The answer is divine love.

With God's love inside us, and God helping us, we can return good for evil done to us. That breaks the vicious downward cycle and also breaks the power of evil to affect us.

Don't tell me this won't work in your case. I have personally heard the victorious testimony of a believer who was tortured by his communist captors yet walked in love and overcame the evil situation. It will work!

Love is stronger than hate. Good is more powerful than evil. You can walk in victory no matter what anyone does to you.

ROMANS 5:5 NIV
5 And hope does not disappoint us, because God has poured out his love into our hearts by the Holy Spirit, whom he has given us.

HEBREWS 13:6 NIV
6 So we say with confidence, "The Lord is my helper; I will not be afraid. What can man do to me?"

SAY THIS: *With God's love, I will overcome evil with good.*

Overcome That Problem You Face

1 JOHN 5:4 NIV
4 for everyone born of God overcomes the world. This is the victory that has overcome the world, even our faith.

Yes, we do face difficulties in life, but they only give us an opportunity to trust the Lord and overcome. Without problems we would have nothing to overcome, and thus not be able to receive all the blessings promised to those who do overcome.

There are seven promises given to overcomers in the second and third chapters of Revelation. Here is the last one:

REVELATION 3:21 NIV
21 To him who overcomes, I will give the right to sit with me on my throne, just as I overcame and sat down with my Father on his throne.

As you face the problems of life, keep your eyes on your destination, just as Jesus did. Walk close to God and depend on Him. He will not fail you.

1 JOHN 4:4 NIV
4 You, dear children, are from God and have overcome them, because the one who is in you is greater than the one who is in the world.

SAY THIS: *I am an overcomer in Christ Jesus. The Lord is my Helper. The One Who is in me is greater than any problem.*

Overcome!

1 JOHN 5:4 NKJ
4 For whatever is born of God overcomes the world. And this is the victory that has overcome the world — our faith.
5 Who is he who overcomes the world, but he who believes that Jesus is the Son of God?

All of us have a choice: we can either make excuses, or make progress in life.

Most people have an excuse. They are too young or old, short or tall, educated or uneducated — whatever. We all have some reason to justify our failure.

But when we focus on God and His ability and willingness to help us in every way — all our excuses beome insignificant.

God's intention is not for His children to be defeated by the problems of life. No! The problems of life are opportunities for us to experience God's help and provision.

God plans for His children to overcome.

How?

By faith!

And faith is available to anyone who will feed on the Bible. Faith comes from God's Word like physical energy comes from eating physical food.

So, if your faith is weak, take in more of God's Word.

Then your faith will grow strong. Then you can overcome the problems you face. Then God will be glorified in you.

SAY THIS: *With the help of God, I will overcome!*

Pray For Our Leaders

1 TIMOTHY 2:1-2 NASB
1 First of all, then, I urge that entreaties and prayers, petitions and thanksgivings, be made on behalf of all men,
2 for kings and all who are in authority, in order that we may lead a tranquil and quiet life in all godliness and dignity.

Praying for our leaders is not a useless ritual. God would not tell us to do something in His Word, unless it would make a difference.

Sometimes, when bad things happen, people ask why God allowed them to happen. But we should be asking ourselves why we allowed them to happen: by not obeying God and praying.

If believers are praying as we ought, we can expect many bad things and difficult times to be avoided.

Since God told us to pray for our leaders, it is our responsibility.

Of course, we shouldn't limit ourselves to praying only for our leaders. We should pray for all people. But we must not forget to pray for our leaders. And not just when we face difficult times, either.

SAY THIS: *Father, I pray that you would give our leaders wisdom, understanding, and insight into all the situations that we face, and the courage to do what is right.*

Pray For Those In Authority

1 TIMOTHY 2:1-2 NASB
1 First of all, then, I urge that entreaties and prayers, petitions and thanksgivings, be made on behalf of all men,
2 for kings and all who are in authority, in order that we may lead a tranquil and quiet life in all godliness and dignity.

Believers have a responsibility to pray for their leaders.

If you live in a country where you have the privilege of voting on your leaders, then you need to take that responsibility seriously, be informed and vote as the Lord directs you.

Don't allow yourself to be swayed by the emotional tactics used in political campaigns, or vote based on your selfish interests. Vote as you believe the Lord would have you to vote. Vote for godly leadership.

But don't stop at voting. Pray for public officials, especially those in high office whose decisions affect many people's lives.

PROVERBS 29:2 LB
2 With good men in authority, the people rejoice; but with the wicked in power, they groan.

SAY THIS: *Father, I pray for godly leaders in our country, and for your blessing on them.*

Day Forty-Nine

Pray Through Daily

Many have criticized the old phrase "praying through," by rightfully telling us that now there is no need to struggle in prayer, since Jesus has already won the battle for us.

The devil is defeated, and any child of God has the right to use the Name of Jesus and immediately be through the devil's resistance and be heard by our Father God.

However, in life we must deal with things of the flesh and this world, which can pry our focus off God.

Spiritually, we can grow dull. It can seem like we are in a fog. Things are not clear. We do not have a note of victory and triumph. We can, and must, press through these impediments.

Pray through — until praying is not hard. Pray until you enjoy it, because you have broken through the things of your flesh and this world that would hold you back from enjoying daily fellowship with your Father God.

> MATTHEW 26:41 NASB
> 41 "Keep watching and praying, that you may not enter into temptation; the spirit is willing, but the flesh is weak."

SAY THIS: *I will "pray through" every day.*

Prayer Strengthens You

ISAIAH 40:31 NKJ
31 But those who wait on the Lord shall renew their strength . . .

Too many people think of prayer only as asking God for what they want. But prayer is much more than that. Prayer is communication and communion with Almighty God. Somehow, in the act of prayer we receive a transfusion of God's strength.

LUKE 22:46 NKJ
46 ". . . pray, lest you enter into temptation."

Being strong enables you to not enter into temptation. Time spent in prayer strengthens you spiritually. (Temptation strikes us all. But we decide whether to yield to the temptation, or not.)

JUDE 1:20 NKJ
20 But you, beloved, building yourselves up on your most holy faith, praying in the Holy Spirit,

According to Jude, praying builds you up, or edifies you. Prayer is a spiritual exercise; the more you do it the stronger you get spiritually.

Some may protest that they don't know how to pray. Just begin to talk to God. And listen for His response, not through a voice, but through His Word, or thoughts in line with His Word. God is not so particular about how His children visit with Him. Just do it!

SAY THIS: *I choose to spend time with God each day in prayer and receive God's strength and help.*

Day Fifty-One

Pride And Selfishness

PHILIPPIANS 2:3-4 NKJ
3 Let nothing be done through selfish ambition or conceit, but in lowliness of mind let each esteem others better than himself.
4 Let each of you look out not only for his own interests, but also for the interests of others.

Pride and selfishness always go together. A truly humble person cannot be selfish.

Pride is self-importance and self-focus — which leads to selfishness which is selfish thinking and selfish acting — the opposite of Jesus' command of agape love in John 13:34.

Pride produces selfishness. All selfishness is a manifestation of pride — thinking you are better, or more important, than others.

Pride is the root of selfishness — and thus the root of all evil. Pride is hidden but manifests as selfish acts.

JAMES 3:16 TEV
16 Where there is jealousy and selfishness, there is also disorder and every kind of evil.

Selfishness causes all evil. All evil proceeds from selfish actions. Selfishness is the only manifest problem, but pride feeds it. Dealing with the root cause of the problem is the only lasting solution.

Submitting to the Lordship of Jesus Christ, and realizing we are not the center of the Universe, is the answer.

Without Jesus, you can do nothing. Apart from His grace, you would not be able to take that next breath of air!

SAY THIS: *Jesus is Lord and I submit to Him.*

Put God First

> MATTHEW 22:37-38 NKJ
> 37 Jesus said to him, "'You shall love the Lord your God with all your heart, with all your soul, and with all your mind.'
> 38 "This is the first and great commandment.

The most important command is to love God with all your being. As with all His commands, God does not give this for His benefit, but for your benefit. Putting God first will bless you, improving your life and well-being.

Loving people, while important, is only secondary according to Jesus. In practice — because God loves people — loving Him will result in you loving people also.

When you get your priority backward — putting people and their needs first — you miss God's plan, and will be relatively ineffective in helping people — compared to what you could have been if you put God first.

> MATTHEW 6:33 CEV
> 33 But more than anything else, put God's work first and do what he wants. Then the other things will be yours as well.

Determine to follow Jesus and obey Him. Don't allow anything other than Jesus Christ to be your highest priority.

SAY THIS: *My highest priority is God. I will put God first in my life.*

Rejoice In The Lord

PHILIPPIANS 4:4 NIV
4 Rejoice in the Lord always. I will say it again: Rejoice!

No matter how bad things are around you, you can always rejoice in the Lord.

God is good — even when circumstances are bad.

You can look beyond the temporary problems of life and focus on the Eternal God and His goodness. You can rejoice that God loves you and that you have a home in Heaven.

If you only rejoice when you feel like it — and circumstances warrant it — you may never rejoice much. But you will miss a lot of joy. For when you rejoice in the Lord and focus on Him, joy begins to flow out of your inner being and strengthens you.

This is God's answer for depression. Focus on God. Rejoice in Him, and receive the spiritual strength you need to carry on in victory.

HABAKKUK 3:18 NIV
18 yet I will rejoice in the LORD, I will be joyful in God my Savior.

"Yet I WILL." Whenever you decide to, you can rejoice. In spite of feelings and circumstances, you can choose to rejoice.

Rejoicing is subject to your will — not your circumstances.

When can you rejoice? When should you rejoice?

1 THESSALONIANS 5:16 NASB
16 Rejoice always;

SAY THIS: *I will rejoice — in the Lord!*

Selfishness

The only thing necessary to change heaven into hell — if God were to allow it — is selfishness.

Selfishness is mankind's fundamental defect. Selfish means: self-centered, self-serving, self-important.

At the root of every problem is selfishness.

> JAMES 3:16 TEV
> 16 Where there is jealousy and selfishness, there is also disorder and every kind of evil.

Every selfish person is potentially your enemy.

All sin is selfish. No one ever sins for someone else — we do it for selfish reasons.

Divine love is the opposite of selfishness. Giving is the opposite of acting selfishly.

We are products of a corrupt culture that teaches selfishness, so it's not unusual for us to think it's not so bad.

But you must die to selfishness — or self-destruct. However, you're unable to change by yourself. You can't change the fruit without changing the root. That's why you must be born again! Only by receiving Jesus Christ and letting Him change you inwardly can you become a truly unselfish person.

No other "religion" teaches to put others first, to love your enemies. Only Christianity teaches you can be totally changed and become a person with a new nature. There is no cure apart from Jesus!

SAY THIS: *Jesus, please cure me of being selfish.*

Sin Hurts

ROMANS 6:23 ICB
23 When someone sins, he earns what sin pays — death. But God gives us a free gift — life forever in Christ Jesus our Lord.

Sin is a teacher whose lessons are hard and painful.

You can't keep your hand in fire without being burned. And you can't sin without hurting people.

Sin harms humans. That's why God classifies it as sin. All sin hurts someone. The reason God is against sin is because He is for people.

Because sin has consequences, it eventually will convince you of the error of sinning — if you live long enough. But why ruin your life finding out what you can know now just by reading the Bible?

God is not a killjoy. His purpose is not to keep the human race from enjoying life.

All that God has written in the Bible is for our benefit. God already knows everything. He gave us the Bible so we could know the truth.

The truth is: sin is bad. Sin hurts.

SAY THIS: *Sin is deadly and I want nothing to do with it.*

Sing A New Song

PSALM 96:1 NIV
1 Sing to the LORD a new song; sing to the LORD, all the earth.

No doubt God, who makes every snowflake different, enjoys new things.

Five times Scripture tells us to sing to the Lord a new song.

You, with God's help, can sing a song to the Lord that's never been sung before.

Don't say you can't do it! God made your mouth and He can give you words to sing.

God is a Creator, and you are His child. Step out in faith. Ask the Lord to help you.

PSALM 105:2 NASB
2 Sing to Him, sing praises to Him; speak of all His wonders.

Get by yourself and practice. Sing a new song. Make it up as you go. If you mess up, God won't laugh at you. It may not be very good. But every parent cherishes their child's first attempts.

Make a joyful noise. Rejoice in the Lord. Both you and the Lord will enjoy it.

EPHESIANS 5:19 NIV
19 ... Sing and make music in your heart to the Lord,

After you practice in private, you may even want to try it in public.

SAY THIS: *I will sing a new song to the Lord.*

Surrounded By Favor

PSALM 5:12 NIV
12 For surely, O LORD, you bless the righteous; you surround them with your favor as with a shield.

God's favor can change your life.

Someone who is favored is called a favor-ite.

(The New Testament teaches that being righteous (in right standing with God), is a gift we receive when we receive Jesus — not something we attain by our works.)

So, the promise of Scripture is that God surrounds you with favor. What does that mean?

Favor is the blessing of God making people like you and treat you well.

Is it automatic? We have access to God's grace only through faith (Romans 5:2). So, you will never experience the fullness of God's favor without believing for it.

Faith is released through words. So every day thank the Lord for giving you favor with people, for surrounding you with favor!

Don't say, "People don't like me." or "Everybody seems to be against me." or "I never get a break."

Instead say, "Thank you Lord for giving me favor with people."

Then watch God begin to move on your behalf!

SAY THIS: *Thank you Lord for surrounding me with favor.*

Talk To Things

> MARK 11:23 NKJ
> 23 "For assuredly, I say to you, whoever says to this mountain, 'Be removed . . . .

Too many people think of the Bible only as a Holy book to be revered. So they put it up on a shelf and make sure no one mistreats it.

But the Bible is a message from God. It gives us instruction for our benefit — practical advice.

It's time to take the Bible down off the pedestal, read it, and act on its instructions.

Here is one seldom acted upon: talk to things.

The devil wants you to think it would be crazy to talk to things. But it's not.

Jesus did it. He talked to sickness. He talked to the storm and told it to be still. He talked to dead bodies and commanded them to get up. He talked to trees. And He talked to the devil and told him to get behind him.

Jesus talked to things. You should too.

You should talk to fear and worry. You should talk to confusion. You should talk to lack. You should talk to sickness. You should talk to the devil. Tell them to leave. Tell them to "be removed."

> LUKE 17:6 NKJ
> 6 So the Lord said, "If you have faith as a mustard seed, you can say to this mulberry tree, 'Be pulled up by the roots and be planted in the sea,' and it would obey you.

SAY THIS: *Jesus said I can talk to things. So I speak to everything that is of the devil and command it to get out of my life now!*

The Benefit Of Prayer

ISAIAH 40:31 NKJ
31 But those who wait on the Lord shall renew their strength; they shall mount up with wings like eagles, they shall run and not be weary, they shall walk and not faint.

Most people look at prayer only as asking God for things. If that defines your prayer life, you are really missing out.

Prayer is communication with God — the greatest privilege on earth.

Prayer is visiting with God. It can include asking for things, but is primarily spending time in God's presence, soaking up His life, His wisdom, and His strength.

Isaiah reveals an important truth to us: those who spend time with God get new strength. Literally, they exchange strength with Him. When we spend time with God He somehow takes away our weakness and replaces it with His strength. What a deal!

As we spend time focused on God, in His presence, we are also changed into His likeness.

2 CORINTHIANS 3:18 NKJ
18 But we all, with unveiled face, beholding as in a mirror the glory of the Lord, are being transformed into the same image . . .

So, if you need more strength to face life, if you want to be more like God, or if you want to develop a closer relationship with the most amazing Being in the universe — prayer is your answer.

Don't worry about knowing the right words or being formal. Just talk to God as you would to a well-respected friend.

SAY THIS: *Excuse me, I think I'll visit with God.*

The Blood Speaks

HEBREWS 12:24 NKJ
24 to Jesus the Mediator of the new covenant, and to the blood of sprinkling that speaks better things than that of Abel.

The Blood testifies that Jesus set us free from all the curse and made us able to partake of the inheritance of the saints. The Blood testifies that Jesus bought our redemption and set us free from the devil.

EPHESIANS 1:7 NIV
7 In him we have redemption through his blood, the forgiveness of sins, in accordance with the riches of God's grace

God worked when the blood of Abel cried unto Him — how much more mightily He will work when it is the blood of His own Son that cries.

By speaking words of faith, we agree with what the Blood says concerning our total and absolute redemption and freedom from the curse.

ROMANS 5:9 NIV
9 Since we have now been justified by his blood, how much more shall we be saved from God's wrath through him!

HEBREWS 9:12 KJV
12 Neither by the blood of goats and calves, but by his own blood he entered in once into the holy place, having obtained eternal redemption for us.

SAY THIS: *Jesus' Blood declares that I am free and forgiven.*

The Cure For Weak Faith

MARK 6:6 NIV
6 And he was amazed at their lack of faith. Then Jesus went around teaching from village to village.

Don't despair if your faith is weak. Everyone starts out with weak faith.

Your faith can be fed and grow strong.

Faith requires evidence to rest upon. The Bible provides the evidence that your faith needs.

ROMANS 10:17 NEW LIFE
17 So then, faith comes to us by hearing the Good News. And the Good News comes by someone preaching it.

Correct teaching on a subject produces faith in your heart.

But it is not enough just to hear teaching on a subject. To keep your faith strong you must feed on scriptures pertaining to that subject, by reading, speaking, and thinking about those scriptures.

And you must exercise your faith for it to grow strong. That is: act on what you learn from Scripture.

Your faith can be strong in one area while being weak in another. For example, most Christians have strong faith concerning the new birth, but weak faith concerning healing, because they have never heard much teaching on the subject of healing.

It is true, as Jesus said in Matthew 4:4, that we need every word that God has spoken — not just some of them.

So, if you want your faith to grow in any area, listen to anointed teaching on that subject, then continue to read, speak, meditate, and act on those scriptures.

SAY THIS: *I will feed my faith on God's Word and it will grow.*

The Gift Of Righteousness

ROMANS 5:17 NIV
17 For if, by the trespass of the one man, death reigned through that one man, how much more will those who receive God's abundant provision of grace and of the gift of righteousness reign in life through the one man, Jesus Christ.

The New Testament reveals the good news that God offers righteousness as a free gift to everyone who receives the Lord Jesus Christ.

Righteousness means right-wise-ness, or being right. So righteousness is right standing, or good standing with God.

Righteousness is a GIFT from God — not something you can earn or achieve. God simply declares that you are innocent, as far as He is concerned, because you believe in Jesus.

You are righteous if Jesus is your Lord. In fact, Jesus is your righteousness. So, you are really as righteous as God is — because He IS your righteousness. As a believer in Jesus, you will never be more righteous — no matter what you do.

1 CORINTHIANS 1:30 NIV
30 It is because of him that you are in Christ Jesus, who has become for us wisdom from God — that is, our righteousness, holiness and redemption.

SAY THIS: *I receive the gift of right standing with God through my Lord Jesus Christ. Thank You Father God for this wonderful gift.*

The Joy Of The Lord Is Your Strength

NEHEMIAH 8:10 NLT
10 . . . Don't be dejected and sad, for the joy of the LORD is your strength!"

I do not claim it is the only meaning, but one thing the Lord showed me from this verse is that our level of joy is like a thermometer revealing our spiritual strength. If our joy is low — our spiritual strength is low. That is because the Lord is our strength, and in His presence there is fullness of joy.

PSALM 16:11 NKJ
11 You will show me the path of life; In Your presence is fullness of joy; At Your right hand are pleasures forevermore.

So, if our joy is low, it means we have not been spending time in God's presence, receiving His strength and help. It means we have got our focus off God and onto something else.

(Although God is always with us, as we worship Him and praise Him and thank Him, God manifests His presence.)

Being gloomy is not a sign of being spiritual. God did not intend for His people to be downcast. Let the world be sad, we have something to rejoice about! Jesus! Heaven!

If you look at your circumstances you may not feel like rejoicing. But if you look at Jesus as He truly is — you will not be able to keep from rejoicing in Him. Jesus is wonderful!

PHILIPPIANS 4:4 NLT
4 Always be full of joy in the Lord. I say it again — rejoice!

SAY THIS: *I will rejoice in the Lord!*

The Message Of Reconciliation

2 CORINTHIANS 5:19 NIV
19 that God was reconciling the world to himself in Christ, not counting men's sins against them. And he has committed to us the message of reconciliation.

The Good News is about reconciliation between God and man. Jesus Christ accomplished it.

Mankind was estranged from God. We had gone our own way, were lost, and couldn't find our way back to fellowship with God. Fortunately, God loved us and did something to help us.

Two extremely important ideas are presented in the above verse.

First, God is not holding people's sins against them! As far as God is concerned, Christ's sacrifice paid the penalty for all sin — and God considers the world reconciled back to Him.

Second, this wonderful good news of what God has done has been committed to us. Human beings must tell it. If we don't — it won't be told.

People can live and die and never know the glorious truth that God is not holding any sins against them — if no one tells them. They need to know they are forgiven, loved by God, and welcome to come back into fellowship with Him through Christ.

Think about this: God is interested in reconciliation. Not in shutting you, or others, out. He is inviting humanity in, saying all is forgiven.

SAY THIS: *Thank You Father God for reconciling me and not holding my sins against me. Please help me to share this message with the right people in the right way.*

The Message Of The New Testament

Mankind has a fatal defect, which manifests as selfishness.

There is a cure — but only one which is effective permanently.

The cure requires injection of new life into your inner being. This life is called eternal life, because it is the life that God, the Eternal One, has.

The cure is free, but the only way to obtain it is to receive and acknowledge Jesus Christ as Lord.

Freedom from this defect requires two things. First, the gift of eternal life, which can be obtained now by receiving the Lord Jesus Christ.

Second, knowing that God loves you greatly — even more than you love yourself.

Therefore, you no longer have to live a self-centered life, worrying about and seeking your own welfare — because you know that God Himself watches out for you.

God will protect you and provide for you — not just enough to barely make it — but an abundant, joy-filled life.

All people who reject this freely offered cure, must soon be placed in quarantine, to be kept from spoiling life for those who do partake of God's cure.

To receive Jesus and His new life, you basically do it the same way you get married. You say: I want to, and I do.

Jesus is listening now, waiting for your decision. He loves you enough to die for you.

SAY THIS: *I receive and acknowledge Jesus Christ as my Lord. Change me, Lord, into what I should be.*

The Ministry Of God

EPHESIANS 4:12 NIV
12 to prepare God's people for works of service, so that the body of Christ may be built up

Ministry means service. To minister is to serve.

How does God "serve us"?

God serves us by helping us. So, primarily, ministry means helping people. Of course, the foremost way of helping people is to help them know God and His Word, so they can receive all God has provided for them.

But anything that helps people — that makes their life easier, or better — is also ministry. That is, it is part of the ministry of God: God's purpose, God's plan, God's desire for humanity.

God desires the best for all people. People were God's idea, and He longs to bless them. God helps people. So, when you help someone, even in the smallest way, you are acting like God.

EPHESIANS 5:1-2 NASB
1 Therefore be imitators of God, as beloved children;
2 and walk in love, just as Christ also loved you, and gave Himself up for us, an offering and a sacrifice to God as a fragrant aroma.

We are to imitate our Father God — or act like Him. How? By walking in love, just as Christ did.

In practical terms, what is walking in love? Helping people. Walking in love means you will help people, you will put their interests first.

When you help people, you are involved in the ministry of God.

SAY THIS: *When I help people, I am serving God.*

Three Keys To A Happy Marriage

(Or, any relationship.)

> JOHN 13:17 KJV
> 17 If ye know these things, happy are ye if ye do them.

1. Be thankful.

It all starts with attitude. If you don't stay on the positive side, failure is inevitable. You cannot have a happy marriage without happy people. Have you noticed that unthankful people are never happy?

2. Express your appreciation.

Let your spouse know by word and deed that you appreciate them. Be specific and lavish in your praise and thanks. Nothing encourages people like encouragement.

People love people who love them. If you want your spouse to love you, the best thing you can do is love them, and let them know it.

3. Aim to please.

If you make them happy, you will be happy. True happiness is never found in trying to please ourselves. Fulfillment comes from accomplishment, and the greatest accomplishment is helping someone else in their life.

SAY THIS: *With God's help, I will have a happy marriage.*

To Become Like Jesus

ROMANS 8:29 NLT
29 For God knew his people in advance, and he chose them to become like his Son, so that his Son would be the firstborn, with many brothers and sisters.

Don't despair over your current condition — you have an amazing destiny!

God's plan is to make you like Jesus Christ. Don't laugh! Remember that nothing is impossible with God.

You WILL be like Jesus!

Always remember that this tops God's agenda for you. You may be concentrating on some temporal project or need in your life. But God's focus is always on transforming you into the likeness of Jesus Christ.

We can't expect becoming like Jesus to always be painless or without difficulty. After all, most of us have quite a few rough edges. But, if we understand what is going on in life, and we keep our eyes on God's goal, it will be easier.

2 CORINTHIANS 4:17-18 NLT
17 For our present troubles are quite small and won't last very long. Yet they produce for us an immeasurably great glory that will last forever!
18 So we don't look at the troubles we can see right now; rather, we look forward to what we have not yet seen. For the troubles we see will soon be over, but the joys to come will last forever.

SAY THIS: *I look forward to God finishing His work in me — making me like Jesus.*

Walk In Love

EPHESIANS 4:31-32 ICB
31 Do not be bitter or angry or mad. Never shout angrily or say things to hurt others. Never do anything evil.
32 Be kind and loving to each other. Forgive each other just as God forgave you in Christ.

As a human who has been hurt, you may find it impossible to forgive and walk in love. But as a child of God, with God helping you, you can do it.

God freely forgave you. Now, with His love placed in your heart, you are to act like Him and forgive others.

EPHESIANS 5:1-2 NIV
1 Be imitators of God, therefore, as dearly loved children
2 and live a life of love, just as Christ loved us and gave himself up for us as a fragrant offering and sacrifice to God.

Putting others first is the essence of walking in love. Selfishness is the opposite of walking in divine love.

COLOSSIANS 3:12-13 NIV
12 Therefore, as God's chosen people, holy and dearly loved, clothe yourselves with compassion, kindness, humility, gentleness and patience.
13 Bear with each other and forgive whatever grievances you may have against one another. Forgive as the Lord forgave you.

If you are having trouble with this, just ask the Lord to work in you and change you. Tell Him you need help.

SAY THIS: *I can walk in love because the Lord is my Helper.*

Watch Your Words

PROVERBS 6:2 NKJ
2 You are snared by the words of your mouth; You are taken by the words of your mouth.

MARK 11:23 NKJ
23 "For assuredly, I say to you . . . he will have whatever he says.

Words are powerful. They are the way humans express their decisions. Words carry authority, even in the spiritual realm.

God created the world with spoken words. Humans are created in the image and likeness of God. Therefore our words also carry authority.

The words you speak are important and carry more weight than you may realize.

Words can get you into trouble. And words can deliver you.

The most powerful and life-giving words in the universe are those spoken by God the Creator.

Fortunately for us, some of what God has said has been written down, for our benefit, in the Bible.

So, we can, and should speak words that are in agreement with what God says. When we do, the power of God is released, because it is God's Word we are speaking.

Remember: whatever God says never loses its power.

SAY THIS: *Please help me Lord to watch my words and speak in agreement with Your Word.*

What You Say Is What You Get

MARK 11:23 NKJ
23 "For assuredly, I say to you, whoever says to this mountain, 'Be removed and be cast into the sea,' and does not doubt in his heart, but believes that those things he says will come to pass, he will have whatever he says.

Jesus said that you will have whatever you say — dependent on believing and not doubting. Think of that. What you say determines what you get in life. It did for the children of Israel. And the Bible says the things which happened to them are lessons for us.

NUMBERS 14:28 NKJ
28 "Say to them, 'As I live,' says the Lord, 'just as you have spoken in My hearing, so I will do to you:

PROVERBS 6:2 NKJ
2 you are snared by the words of your own mouth; you are taken by the words of your mouth.

Words can get you in trouble. And words can deliver you (see Revelation 12:11 and Romans 10:10). Words control your destiny.

All of us face trouble in life and it can sometimes be tempting to wonder why God does not help us sooner and in greater measure. While there is much that we don't understand, we must, on the basis of what Jesus said, realize we are responsible for what happens because of the words we have spoken.

SAY THIS: *Jesus said I will have whatever I say if I believe it.*

When To Rejoice

1 THESSALONIANS 5:16 KJV
16 Rejoice evermore.

1 THESSALONIANS 5:16 NASB
16 Rejoice always;

If you only rejoice when things are perfect, you may not rejoice much in this life.

Why miss out on something so pleasant?

ROMANS 12:12 NRSV
12 Rejoice in hope, be patient in suffering, persevere in prayer.

You can rejoice in hope! That means to rejoice ahead of time.

Why? Because you expect deliverance. You know God's blessing is coming your way — because God is faithful. So rejoice now!

PHILIPPIANS 4:4 NIV
4 Rejoice in the Lord always. I will say it again: Rejoice!

God never changes. He's always good. Focus on Him and you will have something to rejoice about.

SAY THIS: *I will rejoice in the Lord always.*

When You Sin

Sin is deadly. Sin opens the door to the devil.

But none of us are immune to falling into sin. What should we do then?

> 1 JOHN 1:9 NIV
> 9 If we confess our sins, he is faithful and just and will forgive us our sins and purify us from all unrighteousness.

If you sin as a believer, immediately confess it to God. Don't make excuses. You need not beg God to forgive you, because He is a forgiver and has already paid the price so all sin can be forgiven. You confess it to get rid of the sin and its effects on you.

> 1 JOHN 2:1 NIV
> 1 My dear children, I write this to you so that you will not sin. But if anybody does sin, we have one who speaks to the Father in our defense — Jesus Christ, the Righteous One.

Jesus is on your side. His death provided forgiveness for all sins — not just to save sinners, but also forgiveness for believers when we sin. Do not let sin separate you from the Lord and His love. Run to Him and be cleansed. Stay close to Him and receive His help to enable you to not sin.

When you sin, it gives an opportunity for the devil in your life, but God does not turn against you. (God loves all people, even those who sin — and proved it by dying for sinners.) He purposely made provision so you can be cleansed from sin. Jesus' death already paid for your forgiveness. 1 John 1:9 was written to Christians: so when you do sin, confess it — and by faith — immediately receive your cleansing and freedom from all un-righteousness. That shuts the door on the devil.

SAY THIS: *God has made provision for me to be cleansed from sin.*

Who Can Be Against Us?

> ROMANS 8:31 NKJ
> 31 What then shall we say to these things? If God is for us, who can be against us?

We all face opposition. No one likes it. But opposition is a fact of life on earth.

But here's a more important fact: with God for us, opposition doesn't really matter.

With God on our side, what does it matter who opposes us? The worst anyone can do is kill us — which would be doing us a favor. (Being a martyr for Christ and going to be with Him in Heaven is not bad!)

And never forget: God IS for you!

> PSALM 56:9 KJV
> 9 When I cry unto thee, then shall mine enemies turn back: this I know; for God is for me.

> PSALM 118:6-7 LB
> 6 He is for me! How can I be afraid? What can mere man do to me?
> 7 The Lord is on my side; he will help me. Let those who hate me beware.

SAY THIS: *God is for me, so no one can successfully be against me.*

Why Do Christians Fight So Much?

JOHN 13:34-35 NKJ
34 "A new commandment I give to you, that you love one another; as I have loved you, that you also love one another.
35 "By this all will know that you are My disciples, if you have love for one another."

Instead of being known for love, Christians are more likely to be known for disagreements and fighting with other Christians.

Why?

Those who fight are displaying their immaturity. Children can be expected to squabble over insignificant things, but adults should not.

Yet even Christian leaders often fight with other Christian leaders.

It is the devil's strategy to get believers in strife because it opens the door to him. Do you really want to open the door to the devil?

JAMES 3:16 KJV
16 For where envying and strife is, there is confusion and every evil work.

God allows us to face the temptation of strife so we can overcome and learn to walk in love. We are continually given the opportunity to walk in love.

God's primary concern now is preparing us to inhabit eternity with Him. His plan is to make us like Jesus (Romans 8:29). To become like Jesus, we must learn to resist the temptation to not walk in love.

SAY THIS: *With God's help, I will walk in love. I refuse to fight and be in strife with other Christians.*

Why Read The Bible?

"I'm a busy person. I have a lot to do. Why should I spend my time reading the Bible? I don't have time to do all I need to do as it is."

"I already believe in Jesus Christ, that He's the Son of God and my Savior. I've already heard the Gospel."

"Why should I read the Bible?"

Please think about the following Scriptures. Then, you will understand why you should read the Bible.

> JOHN 8:31-32 RSV
> 31 Jesus then said to the Jews who had believed in him, "If you continue in my word, you are truly my disciples,
> 32 and you will know the truth, and the truth will make you free."
>
> JOHN 14:23-24 RIEU
> 23 Jesus replied: 'If anyone loves me he will cherish my word; my Father will love him and we will come to him and make him our abode.
> 24 He that does not love me neglects my words. Yet the word you hear is not my own but that of the Father who sent me.
>
> ACTS 20:32 NKJ
> 32 "So now, brethren, I commend you to God and to the word of His grace, which is able to build you up and give you an inheritance among all those who are sanctified.

SAY THIS: *I will read and study the Bible.*

Words Are Spiritual Weapons

REVELATION 12:11 NKJ
11 "And they overcame him by the blood of the Lamb and by the word of their testimony, and they did not love their lives to the death.

Words are more important than most people realize. All authority is exercised through words.

When it comes to overcoming the enemy of our souls, and all his tactics, we must speak words of faith in line with the Bible.

What Jesus did for you is enough. He defeated the devil for you. However, you must enforce that defeat by speaking and standing in agreement with God. Only then will you see Jesus' victory manifest in your life.

EPHESIANS 6:17 NKJ
17 And take the helmet of salvation, and the sword of the Spirit, which is the word of God;

A sword is a weapon. God's Word is not a weapon when laying on your coffee table. It only becomes a spiritual weapon when you speak it in faith.

You must take it. Your spiritual weapon is speaking the Word of God. You must take the Word and speak it — just like Jesus did.

SAY THIS: *I overcome by what Jesus did, and my words that enforce that victory over the devil.*

Words Bring Success

JOSHUA 1:8 NKJ
8 "This Book of the Law shall not depart from your mouth, but you shall meditate in it day and night, that you may observe to do according to all that is written in it. For then you will make your way prosperous, and then you will have good success.

God's Word never changes. What God promised would work for Joshua will work for you, also. The problem with most of us is that we are just too busy to put God's Word first like we should. But we are not too busy to work trying to get ahead. Explain that.

God never lies. Follow His instructions given above and you WILL have prosperity and good success. Maybe not in 10 minutes. Maybe not even for 10 years. But you will. God promises it.

Notice that Joshua 1:8 does not just say to think about God's Word. No — the Word must continually be in your mouth! Words!

1 PETER 3:10 NKJ
10 For "He who would love life and see good days, let him refrain his tongue from evil, and his lips from speaking guile;

Speaking and thinking in line with God's Word will cause you to prosper and succeed. If you would like to see good days, the Bible admonishes you to watch your words!

Never confess defeat. Confessing Jesus as Lord of every situation brings glory to God.

SAY THIS: *I will keep God's Word in my thoughts and in my mouth. Then I will have good success in life.*

Day Seventy-Nine

Words Control Your Life

PROVERBS 18:20-21 NKJ
20 A man's stomach shall be satisfied from the fruit of his mouth, and from the produce of his lips he shall be filled.
21 Death and life are in the power of the tongue, and those who love it will eat its fruit.

Proverbs 18:20 says what your lips produce will fill your life. Your lips produce — words.

Words determine the course and the outcome of your life. You now have, and will continue to have, the fruit your tongue produces.

To change your life you need to change your words.

JAMES 3:2,8 NIV
2 We all stumble in many ways. If anyone is never at fault in what he says, he is a perfect man, able to keep his whole body in check.
8 but no man can tame the tongue. It is a restless evil, full of deadly poison.

To change the words you speak you need God's help.

As Jesus said, out of the abundance of your heart your mouth will speak. So, you need a new heart and you need it filled with God's Word. Only in that way can your tongue be brought under complete control.

SAY THIS: *Lord, because your Word teaches that words control my life, please help me to control my words.*

You Are A Citizen of Heaven

PHILIPPIANS 3:20 NRSV
20 But our citizenship is in heaven, and it is from there that we are expecting a Savior, the Lord Jesus Christ.

As a believer in Jesus Christ, you have a new citizenship. Your name is written in Heaven. Heaven is your homeland.

Because you are its citizen, Heaven is responsible for you. If necessary, Heaven will send its soldiers (angels) to assist you, and when necessary, to evacuate you.

Although we live on earth, we operate under the laws of our homeland, Heaven, as well as the laws of earth.

As a citizen you have certain rights and obligations. To understand them you need to read the Bible with the help of illumination by the Holy Spirit. You need to ask the Lord to teach you and give you understanding of these things.

COLOSSIANS 1:13 NRSV
13 He has rescued us from the power of darkness and transferred us into the kingdom of his beloved Son,

As believers, we are no longer under the authority or control of the devil. We have been transferred into a new kingdom.

One of our rights as citizens of Heaven is to resist the devil and all his works. Anything that is of the devil, we do not have to submit to.

SAY THIS: *I am a citizen of Heaven. Jesus is my Lord and King!*

Day Eighty-One

You Are God's Garden

1 CORINTHIANS 3:9 LB
9 We are only God's coworkers. You are God's garden, not ours; you are God's building, not ours.

We discovered that God's Word is a seed (Luke 8:11). Now we see that the Bible says that we, as believers, are God's garden — the place where seed is planted.

The question for you to consider is: who determines the harvest? God, or you?

(The harvest I speak of is the fruit, or result, of the Word of God. The harvest of blessing that God's Word produces in your life.)

I suggest that the harvest is mainly controlled by the one who determines what seed is planted. Would you agree?

If wheat seed is planted, it is unreasonable to expect a harvest of corn. If only a few seeds are planted, it is unreasonable to expect a large harvest. Wouldn't you agree?

Yes, you are God's field, but He allows you a lot of freedom to choose what will be produced in your life. And the main way you choose is by choosing what seed will be planted in your heart and mind.

You can choose something other than God's Word. You can also choose different areas of God's Word. Planting different scriptures will produce different results in your life.

If all you ever plant are scriptures on the new birth, you cannot expect to have a huge harvest of healing or financial blessing in your life. The choice is yours.

SAY THIS: *I am God's garden. Lord, help me plant the seed of your Word in me in abundance.*

You Are God's Work Of Art

EPHESIANS 2:10 NLT
10 For we are God's masterpiece. He has created us anew in Christ Jesus, so that we can do the good things he planned for us long ago.

Outwardly, you may not appear to be much of a masterpiece. You may think you look like a piece of junk. But inwardly, and in reality, you are God's work of art — and God does not make any junk.

All that is outward and seen is only temporary — like the cocoon the butterfly inhabits for only a short time. So, while you should take care of your present body, don't be overly concerned about it. Most importantly, don't think of yourself as just the body you are now living in.

You are a child of Almighty God, creator and ruler of the universe. Someone God is "raising" to be His companion for eternity. You are NOT insignificant.

Admittedly, you are a work in progress. God still has more work to do with you — but He is the artist, and He will finish His work. (Hint: as you submit to God, the easier it is for Him to change you into the wonderful image He has in mind.)

Someday, everyone will clearly see what God has done in you: making you a wonderful, unique individual worthy of Himself.

SAY THIS: *Regardless of how I look or feel, I AM God's work of art — His masterpiece.*

You Are Not A Failure

EPHESIANS 2:10 NIV
10 For we are God's workmanship, created in Christ Jesus to do good works, which God prepared in advance for us to do.

You may have failed, but you are not a failure.

It is not the essence of what and who you are. Failure is just something that happened to you.

God created you, and He made you able to do good. Maybe you have not yet discovered what you were created for, but God has a plan for you. When you fit into God's plan you will find that God truly made you "a work of His art."

A donkey could compare itself to a race horse and think it was a failure. But a donkey was created for other things than running fast.

Find out what you were created to be and do. Then rejoice as you do it.

SAY THIS: *I am God's unique work of art — still in progress.*

You Are Not An Orphan

JOHN 14:18 NIV
18 I will not leave you as orphans; I will come to you.

You are not facing life all alone — no matter how you feel.

Jesus is with you. He promised to never forsake you.

Our enemy loves to make us think we have no help, that God does not care, and we have no hope. But the devil is a liar.

"But why does God allow things to look so bleak? Why doesn't He help me sooner?"

God desires faith and trust from us. Without testing times we would have no opportunity to show our faith. Without obstacles we would have nothing to overcome.

We must always remember that God is raising a family, preparing us for eternity with Him. It can be a great error to judge everything by "the bottom line" today.

We must trust our Father God, because only He really knows what the "true bottom line" is. And we can trust Him, because He is good and trustworthy.

SAY THIS: *Thank you Father God that I am not facing life all alone — as an orphan. You are my Father and are taking good care of me. I trust You — for time and eternity.*

You Are Part Of Christ's Body On Earth

1 CORINTHIANS 12 NLT
12 The human body has many parts, but the many parts make up only one body. So it is with the body of Christ.
17 Suppose the whole body were an eye — then how would you hear? Or if your whole body were just one big ear, how could you smell anything?
18 But God made our bodies with many parts, and he has put each part just where he wants it.
21 The eye can never say to the hand, "I don't need you." The head can't say to the feet, "I don't need you."
22 In fact, some of the parts that seem weakest and least important are really the most necessary.
27 Now all of you together are Christ's body, and each one of you is a separate and necessary part of it.

Scripture says we are a Body — not just that we are "like a body." You ARE connected to everyone who acknowledges Jesus Christ as Lord — whether you like them, or think they are necessary, or not. Whatever happens to ANY member of the Body does have an affect on EVERY member.

Remember this the next time you are tempted to speak ill of another believer, or mistreat them. Even if they don't believe exactly like you, or go to the same church — they are still connected to you in Christ. So be nice to your Body!

SAY THIS: *I am a member of Christ's Body on earth. Today I will let Jesus Christ manifest His love and wisdom through me.*

You Can Do All Things Through Christ

PHILIPPIANS 4:13 NKJ
13 I can do all things through Christ who strengthens me.

God often makes statements in the Bible that go against what we feel like, or what it looks like to us at the time.

God is trying to move us to a higher plane of faith where we depend on Him and not on what we feel like.

Others try to evade the issue by saying that a verse only applies to someone else — like the Apostle Paul — not to them.

Well, if you don't believe, you won't receive help. But help is available. And that help and strength is just as available to you as it was to the Apostle Paul, because the Lord does not play favorites.

Paul didn't say, "I can do all things because I am an apostle." No, it is "through Christ" that he was enabled to do what he needed to do. And you, as a believer, are in Christ just as much as the Apostle Paul was.

You choose. Either step out in faith in God and say you can do it with His help, and watch God raise you up to that level. Or, cower back in fear, and say you cannot do it.

SAY THIS: *I CAN do all things through Christ who strengthens me.*

You Don't Face Life All Alone

JOHN 14:18 BARCLAY
18 I will not leave you to face life all alone. I am coming to you.

Being alone — with no help — is a horrible feeling. One the devil would love for you to believe is your lot.

You are NOT alone! Jesus promised!

When you feel alone, desolate, and helpless — remember the promises of Jesus.

HEBREWS 13:5 NIV
5 . . . God has said, "Never will I leave you; never will I forsake you."

Your feelings are not the true test of reality. God cannot lie. He is with you now, whether you feel like it, or whether it looks like it, or not.

Since God is always with you, it would be rude to always ignore Him. So call on Him and discuss things with Him. Let God be your friend. That's His plan.

SAY THIS: *I am not facing life all alone. God is with me.*

You Have A Purpose

> 2 TIMOTHY 1:9 NKJ
> 9 who has saved us and called us with a holy calling, not according to our works, but according to His own purpose and grace which was given to us in Christ Jesus before time began,

You have a purpose in life, a job to do, a mission to fulfill.

You are here for a reason.

What is it?

Ask God. He knows.

> EPHESIANS 1:11 NIV
> 11 In him we were also chosen, having been predestined according to the plan of him who works out everything in conformity with the purpose of his will,

Of course, I can only answer that question in general terms.

If you are a parent, raising your child is important. Helping a friend is important. You never know how your actions may affect the world — even through helping just one person.

Don't just wait around for some "big purpose" — for with God all the details are important — even the "small" ones.

If you don't know your purpose, just do whatever you can to help the people around you. Through that, and walking with God, you will accomplish your purpose.

SAY THIS: *I was born for a purpose. God has a plan for me.*

Your Body Is Your House

> 2 CORINTHIANS 5:1 NKJ
> 1 For we know that if our earthly house, this tent, is destroyed, we have a building from God, a house not made with hands, eternal in the heavens.

The "real you" is not your body. Your body is just a house you live in so you can function here on earth.

Just as someone can change houses where they live, you can, and will someday, leave your body and still exist.

We focus too much on our body. The inner part of us is most important. These bodies we live in are not eternal.

It is not wrong to take care of our bodies, any more than it is wrong to take care of the house or apartment where we live. It is a mistake, however, to spend all our time on our body and neglect our spirit and mind.

> 1 TIMOTHY 4:8 RSV
> 8 for while bodily training is of some value, godliness is of value in every way, as it holds promise for the present life and also for the life to come.

Who a person is on the inside is more important than what their body looks like.

We judge too often on the house (body) that people live in, instead of focusing on the real person living inside that body.

SAY THIS: *My body is only a temporary house where I live.*

Your Hairs Are Numbered

LUKE 12:7 NIV
7 Indeed, the very hairs of your head are all numbered. Don't be afraid; you are worth more than many sparrows.

Have you ever wondered how God has time to keep count of how many hairs you have today?

God probably built a program into your brain that tracks your total hair count, which He can quickly scan without having to spend much time on your hair. (Your life might also be better if you spent less time worrying about your hair.)

Or, maybe we each have a hair angel assigned to keep our current hair count.

The point is not that God spends all His time counting hairs, but that there is nothing about you God is not fully aware of at all times.

If your hair count is important enough for God to monitor — however He does it — surely He monitors everything else that concerns you, also.

Think of that! God is aware of the smallest detail of everything in life that affects you. It matters to Him.

You are His child. Every detail of your life concerns God.

Knowing that, Jesus said, "Don't be afraid."

SAY THIS: *God keeps current on every detail of my life.*

You Can Receive Forgiveness

Sin hurts people. That is why God is against sin, because He loves people.

The good news is, whether you are a Christian believer, or not, you can receive forgiveness for all your sins today.

If you have sinned as a Christian, the Bible is clear on what you should do, and what the Lord will do.

> 1 JOHN 1:9 NLT
> 9 But if we confess our sins to him, he is faithful and just to forgive us our sins and to cleanse us from all wickedness.

God has already provided for forgiveness of all sins through the sacrifice of Jesus. We do not have to convince God to forgive us. It was His idea. All we have to do is agree with God that we did sin, and receive His forgiveness. God has already declared that forgiveness is ours, we just have to come to Him by faith, trusting His Word, and receive it.

The Bible places no limits, or restrictions, on how often we can be forgiven. In fact, Jesus indicated we should forgive others in an unlimited manner, so we know God would not do any less than He asks of us.

> MATTHEW 18:21-22 NLT
> 21 Then Peter came to him and asked, "Lord, how often should I forgive someone who sins against me? Seven times?"
> 22 "No, not seven times," Jesus replied, "but seventy times seven!

All human beings have sinned. We have all fallen short and need a Savior. It is only by God's grace and His forgiveness that anyone can be right with God.

> ROMANS 6:23 NLT
> 23 For the wages of sin is death, but the free gift of God is eternal life through Christ Jesus our Lord.

We can be glad because Jesus Christ came to save sinners, and He paid the price for the forgiveness of all sins by shedding His blood. No matter how badly you have sinned, you can receive forgiveness today. In fact, God has already forgiven you. He is just waiting on you to come to Him and receive that forgiveness, so you can be in right standing with Him as a free gift. This is Good News because sin produces death and we all need a Savior.

> ROMANS 5:17 NLT
> 17 For the sin of this one man, Adam, caused death to rule over many. But even greater is God's wonderful grace and his gift of righteousness, for all who receive it will live in triumph over sin and death through this one man, Jesus Christ.

Jesus paid the price in full for your complete forgiveness and cleansing from all sin — no matter what you have done. You can be done with it and put it in the past today. Not only can you be forgiven of all your sins, but God will work in you to change you and enable you to overcome those sins that have trapped you in the past. With God's help you can overcome! You can be free from the power of sin to control you!

> ROMANS 3:19-28 NLT
> 19 Obviously, the law applies to those to whom it was given, for its purpose is to keep people from having excuses, and to show that the entire world is guilty before God.
> 20 For no one can ever be made right with God by doing what the law commands. The law simply shows us how sinful we are.
> 21 But now God has shown us a way to be made right with him without keeping the requirements of the law, as was promised in

the writings of Moses and the prophets long ago.
22 We are made right with God by placing our faith in Jesus Christ. And this is true for everyone who believes, no matter who we are.
23 For everyone has sinned; we all fall short of God's glorious standard.
24 Yet God, with undeserved kindness, declares that we are righteous. He did this through Christ Jesus when he freed us from the penalty for our sins.
25 For God presented Jesus as the sacrifice for sin. People are made right with God when they believe that Jesus sacrificed his life, shedding his blood. This sacrifice shows that God was being fair when he held back and did not punish those who sinned in times past,
26 for he was looking ahead and including them in what he would do in this present time. God did this to demonstrate his righteousness, for he himself is fair and just, and he declares sinners to be right in his sight when they believe in Jesus.
27 Can we boast, then, that we have done anything to be accepted by God? No, because our acquittal is not based on obeying the law. It is based on faith.
28 So we are made right with God through faith and not by obeying the law.

ROMANS 5:6-11 NLT
6 When we were utterly helpless, Christ came at just the right time and died for us sinners.
7 Now, most people would not be willing to die for an upright person, though someone might perhaps be willing to die for a person who is especially good.
8 But God showed his great love for us by sending Christ to die for us while we were still sinners.
9 And since we have been made right in God's sight by the blood of Christ, he will certainly save us from God's condemnation.
10 For since our friendship with God was restored by the death of

his Son while we were still his enemies, we will certainly be saved through the life of his Son.

11 So now we can rejoice in our wonderful new relationship with God because our Lord Jesus Christ has made us friends of God.

ROMANS 10:9-10 NLT
9 If you confess with your mouth that Jesus is Lord and believe in your heart that God raised him from the dead, you will be saved. 10 For it is by believing in your heart that you are made right with God, and it is by confessing with your mouth that you are saved.

JOHN 1:12 NLT
12 But to all who believed him and accepted him, he gave the right to become children of God.

Jesus is the friend of sinners, and He will receive anyone who comes to Him. You don't have to be perfect for Jesus to receive you. You just have to receive Him. Then He will save you and make you a child of God.

As Romans 10:9-10 reveals, speaking words, declaring that you put your trust in Jesus Christ and receive Him as Lord, is how you receive Jesus. In that sense, it is similar to getting married: you say "I do" and you make it publicly known.

If you have made this decision, please let us know through our web site: www.ChurchForAll.org

Ordering Information

This book may be purchased through www.amazon.com. Additional information on ordering may be available at:

www.CFApublications.com

If you were helped, enlightened, or encouraged by reading this book, please consider leaving your comments about this book at www.amazon.com so others will be encouraged to read it, too.

www.ingramcontent.com/pod-product-compliance
Lightning Source LLC
Chambersburg PA
CBHW031258290426
44109CB00012B/630